Leisure Arts

Painting
Landscapes
in Watercolour

Jan Burridge

SEARCH PRESS

Wellwood North Farm Road Tunbridge Wells

Making a start

Observation, concentration and patience are needed for successful watercolour painting. In this book I explain some of my own techniques, but these three qualities are essential.

The most attractive aspect of painting in watercolour is that you need very little paint to obtain interesting effects of light and luminosity. But you have to control the density and flow of pigment and water on paper if you want good results.

On the other hand, excessive attention to detail would make a painting look hesitant or overworked.

I assume that you are interested in painting landscapes, and that your materials are of the best quality that you can afford. On that assumption, you should begin by studying the behaviour of water and pigment on paper.

There is a colour-mixing chart on page 4. The effects of colours mixed in a paintbox are very different from those of colours overlaid on one another on paper. When mixing paint in a paintbox, try not to make the paint too thick. The chart on page 4 also shows the gradations of each colour as more water is added. You will see that some colours remain fairly opaque whereas others wash out very easily. This chart shows the colours with which I paint. Try making a similar chart in colours of your own choice; mix them in the paintbox and gradate them on paper. Try making the same chart with overlaid washes of colour; you will see, for example, the different effects of yellow overlaid on blue and blue overlaid on yellow.

On page 10 there is a black-and-white brushstroke chart. Experiment with each example but use mixed colours or more than one colour. Examine the results for opacity, evenness of wash and luminosity.

Try a simple watercolour sketch like that on page 10 and aim to use all the different techniques in the examples on that page. If you take care, you can produce strong effects in a short time.

The watercolour sketching demonstration on pages 28–9 requires quick, efficient brushwork that is no more difficult than that of the examples on page 10.

In this book I show landscape sketches made under varying lighting and weather conditions. I painted the

demonstrations that precede each painting when the
work was finished, in order to show how each painting
was constructed. There are minor disparities between
each stage which do not affect the main point of each
demonstration.

Chart to show colour mixing and staining power

	Ultramarine	Prussian blue	Yellow ochre	Raw umber	Burnt sienna	Sepia
Yellow ochre						
Sap green						
Windsor green						
Ultramarine						
Prussian blue						
Crimson						
Sepia						

Detail from the finished painting on page 9

These two skies are from the finished paintings on pages 9 and 13. Although the colours used are quite similar, the brushwork is very different. The sky in the top painting is flat and even, requiring a wet-into-wet wash with no hard edges. The rainy sky has deeper colour that has been left to dry and then disturbed with a wet brush to give heavy rain clouds.

On a summer's day

A landscape in warm summer sunshine under a clear bright sky is a very attractive subject for watercolour painting. The light reflected from the surroundings produces vivid colours, and deep contrasting shadows result in bold lines within the landscape. Although these conditions are most attractive, they are not necessarily the easiest to reproduce in watercolour as you need experience to handle rich colours and strong shapes sensitively. I painted the landscape shown on page 9 on a glorious late summer afternoon. The trees were just beginning to show a hint of magnificent autumn shades; the grass was thick and rich in colour; and the river was dark and deep under the trees but bright with reflected light in the open.

I was sitting on a river bank looking downstream. The sun was slightly to the right in front of me and glinting through foliage which shaded me from its bright light. The sky was cloudless and the sunlight very strong, giving intense contrast between areas of light reflected by the water on my left and the grassy slopes of the far bank and the deep shadows under the trees and bridge. The church tower appeared as a soft shadow against the sky to the left of the trees above the other bank.

Demonstration

Size: 353 × 253 mm/14 × 10 in. Paper: Bockingford 285 gsm/140 lb. Brushes: 0, 1, 2 sable.

Stage 1

Before painting, make a sketch to establish the correct proportions of the features in the landscape. You can also use this drawing to isolate areas of dark and light tone and to make pencil notes on colour strengths. When painting I prefer to finish one area at a time. With a subject like this, I usually begin with the sky.

Make a very fine pencil drawing to isolate the sky shapes against the landscape. Wet the sky area and put in washes in different shades of French ultramarine, cobalt green and yellow ochre. Remember that a wash always dries paler so allow for it at this stage. The results are never satisfactory if you go over a wash once it has been allowed to dry. While the wash is still wet, add a little more yellow ochre around the outline of the trees to indicate the powerful sunlight coming from behind the leaves.

Mix a thin wash of Prussian blue, crimson lake and sepia, and paint in the silhouette of the church. Distance and shadow combine to conceal all architectural details on the church except for a row of parapets that catch the angle of the sun along the roof. Highlight these with yellow ochre. Let the sky and the church dry completely.

Stage 2

Begin painting the brightly-lit grass on the far bank by laying in a wash of sap green, hooker's green and raw umber. Do not let these three colours intermix too much or the subtle changes in colour will be indistinct. Insert the trees on the left with a mixture of sap green, sepia and Prussian blue. Give warmth to the turning copper beech leaves on the tree to the right of the

Stage 1

Stage 2

Stage 3

Stage 4

church with a mixture of sepia, burnt umber and crimson lake. Use some drybrush here to give harder edges and suggest branches and finer detail.

Stage 3

Paint the tree at the water's edge with a mixture of sepia, sap green and burnt sienna. Use the same mixture with a touch of Prussian blue for foliage on the tree on the right. Use wet-into-wet and drybrush on these trees to obtain differing textures and hard and soft edges to the foliage. The trunks of these two trees call for differing approaches: the tree at the water's

edge has darker lines down the side of the trunk which make it far more prominent than the trunk of the right-hand tree.

Use a pale wash of sepia and raw umber for the bridge. Let this wash dry before adding more shadows and architectural details with a mixture of crimson lake and Prussian blue.

Stage 4

The dark areas of water below the bridge reflect the tree and bank beside it. Use the same colours (sap green, hooker's green, raw umber, sepia and Prussian

Stage 5 - the finished painting

blue) to lay in the darkest areas on the surface of the water. A few horizontal brushstrokes will give distance to the water.

Stage 5

When these colours are dry, use raw umber and sap green and some drybrush to show the weed and lilies floating on the river. Some remaining areas of white paper give the effect of broken reflected light. Put in thin washes of sap green and hooker's green for the grassy bank on the right and lay secondary washes of wet-into-wet into this to give darker areas of grass. Use

these colours for the reeds in the foreground and add dead vegetation in sepia and raw umber, and a little Prussian blue for the shadows. Wet the lightest area of the river and put in an extremely pale wash of cobalt blue; add a few reflection details to this water surface. Use drybrush for the sharper details and wet-into-wet for soft dark shadowy areas.

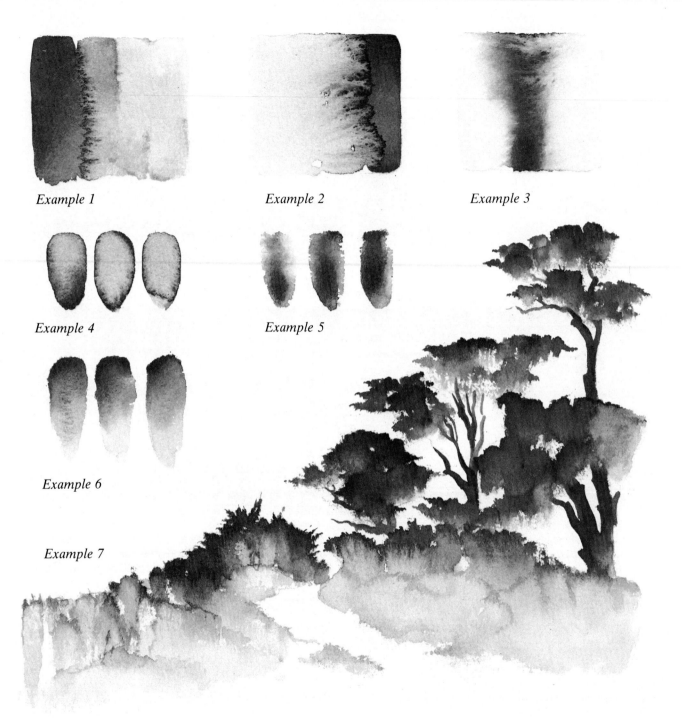

Example 1

Example 2

Example 3

Example 4

Example 5

Example 6

Example 7

10

Gloomy weather

Washes that diffuse too widely into one another or develop an overall evenness of tone quickly destroy the freshness and light of a painting.

Practise wash control so that you can predict the flow pattern of pigment as brushwork dries. Above are a few simple demonstrations which you can practise and which will also help to paint "Gloomy Weather".

Example 1

Use a flat brush to produce a stroke of colour on dry paper; with a clean brush immediately add three strokes of water on the right-hand side. Watch how the colour is carried across the entire area as it dries.

Example 2

Paint three strokes of water with a clean brush and add one stroke of colour to the right of these. Look at the difference between the results and those of example 1.

Example 3

Paint three strokes of clear water and then put one brushstroke of colour in the middle of these three strokes. Watch the paint disperse softly, leaving no hard edges within the wash area. These three basic tests help you to predict the flow of colour across a sky or a large wash area. With care and practice, you can judge the right softness or colour accent to define the edges of cloud banks for large, even-toned landscape areas.

Example 4

Take a large, pointed sable brush and make a single stroke of colour. Wash the brush and add a brush-load of clean water to the stroke; study the result.

Example 5

This is the reverse of example 4. Make a stroke on the paper with clean water and then add a brush loaded with paint to this clear brushstroke. Notice that the colour is richest at the centre of the mark and lightest at the edge.

Example 6

Load your brush with water and dip the tip in pigment before making a stroke on the paper, so that you push the main concentration of colour towards the top of the stroke. This technique is very useful for trees and grasses, as in example 7.

Demonstration

Size: 265 × 215 mm/10½ × 8½ in. Brushes. 0, 1, 2 sable. Paper: Bockingford 285 gms/140 lb.

I was going for a walk on an extremely wet summer's day when I came across this view. The sky was very heavy and a light rain was falling. The sun was beginning to break through the clouds far out to sea, giving a dramatic light effect.

Each stage has been isolated for the purposes of this demonstration. However, with a painting that has as many soft-edged washes as this, you should maintain a continuous flow of work. In this way washes merge with one another when still wet and create an overall impression of softness and dampness in the air. If each wash is allowed to dry separately, hard lines of colour appear at the edges and the more subtle muted effects are destroyed. This painting took me thirty-five minutes from start to finish.

Stage 1

Wash in the heavy cloud with a mixture of Prussian blue and crimson, using a wide flat-wash brush. Keep the lower edges of this wash wet to allow the paint to merge with the clouds in the distance.

Stage 1

Stage 2

Stage 3

Stage 4

Stage 2

Paint in the distant clouds with a broken wash made up of ultramarine, turquoise and yellow ochre. Although there is a lot of water on the paper at this stage, keep to a hard-edge horizontal line for the horizon; do not make all the cloud edges soft. The sea reflects the sky, so add bands of Prussian blue in the water with

horizontal areas of white paper. When dry, lay a very pale wash of yellow ochre across part of these.

Stage 3

Position the line of trees in the middle distance, using sepia, burnt umber and Prussian blue. Paint these loosely on dry paper so that the tops are silhouetted sharply against the distant sea. Wet the lower edges to

Stage 5 - the finished painting

encourage the paint to merge softly with the fore-ground foliage in stage 4.

Stage 4

To create an impression of soft wet grass, lay in a loose broken wash of hooker's green, burnt sienna, yellow ochre and sap green.

Stage 5

To add further detail to the foreground grasses, work some pale wash lines on dry paper. The sharp edges produced make the grasses appear very close and put the trees and other vegetation further into the distance. Lift some of the colour from the trees with tissues to give a misty impression.

When looking for landscape compositions, it is often good to concentrate on a single attractive object. I made this sketch of an old tree because of its interesting shape which heightened the atmosphere of a simple landscape overcast by a dramatic sky.

Beside the wall

It is often helpful to base a landscape composition on an interesting detail, such as an attractive gate, a stone wall, a building, or a fallen tree. Then you have a focal point from which the eye can travel to distant parts of the picture; the device also helps you to extend the field of focus to include individual leaves, flowers and grasses.

When planning a painting, do not make too large a jump from the focal point at the centre to the background behind, or the painting will lack harmony. Balance colour as well as composition. The nearer the focal object, the more critical its position in the painting *and* its related colour values.

Demonstration

Size: 265 × 265 mm/10½ × 10½ in.
Brushes: 0, 1, 2, 6 sable. Paper: Bockingford 285 gsm/ 140 lb.

Stage 1

This ancient stone stile is an ideal focal feature and a natural bridge from the late evening sky behind the distant trees to the brambles in the right foreground. Wet the sky area, but not right up to the edges of all the natural subjects. Mix a wash of yellow ochre with a touch of hooker's green and draw around the edge of the wet area so that the colour spreads inwards and diffuses evenly. Let the wash dry.

Stage 2

For the golden-brown trees in the distance, paint burnt sienna and sepia in drybrush. The dark-green conifers are a wash of sap green, hooker's green and sepia with lots of water. To give them varied tone, first paint the outline of each tree, then add water to the centre of the tree.

Stage 3

The wall on the left is not difficult to paint. Use a very fine brush to draw the outline of the stones in sepia.

Keep the paint thin, and try to capture the shape of the stones so that they look like heavy rocks and not grey, weightless blobs. When the paint is dry, add raw umber, sepia and hooker's green in drybrush to give the effect of ancient moss and lichen.

I always mix at least two colours when painting outlines. One colour produces a flat, dull and (for landscape painting) unreal effect.

The light-grey wash used for the stile has a base of sepia with Prussian blue and crimson red added and drybrushed in places to give texture and roughness to the surface. Leave some small areas of white paper for highlights. Draw a grain on the wooden rail above the stile so that it has a different texture to the stone.

Stage 4

For the dark foliage to the right of the stile brush in sepia, hooker's green and touches of raw umber and Prussian blue. Do not push the paint around too much or it will become muddy. Let small areas dry so that hard edges give good colour variety in the area of shadow.

Use a no. 6 sable brush for the grass in the left foreground. Vary the colours: sap green, raw umber and burnt sienna, and use some drybrush to give a variety of forms.

Stage 5 (shown in detail on page 32)

Complete the vegetation and the lower tree trunk by drawing around their shapes with sepia. Take great care when doing this; study the leaves and stems so that you make the plants look like brambles and cow parsley. Take a larger sable than the one used for the basic drawing, load it with water and fade the outlines of these plants into the background so that it matches the dark foliage of stage 4. Use thin yellow ochre mixed with crimson red for the bramble stems, and mix sap and hooker's green in different proportions for the younger leaves. Use sepia and Prussian blue for the older leaves.

If you imagine the finished painting without these close foreground details, it appears flat.

Stage 1

Stage 2

Stage 3

Stage 4

Stage 5 - the finished painting

Light snow

Winter with its many transformations of light and colour demands different techniques from painting in summer. In winter sunlight is weaker and the low angle of the rays forms long blue shadows. When stripped of their foliage, trees have fascinating outlines, particularly when they are laced with heavy frosts or a fresh fall of snow. Trunks and branches appear darker and the warm yellow-greens and golden-browns of summer foliage are gone. Winter colours are flatter and less vibrant; they are usually cold shades of blue-green and grey with a little pink in distant trees and long shadows.

In the depths of winter, the brilliant reflective surface of snow emphasizes and distorts colours and details; if the sun shines, snow produces perhaps the brightest light in the whole year. Otherwise it affords very soft, almost indiscernible variations in shadow. Leave fairly small areas of paper completely white when painting snow. Use very pale washes of colour to produce undulations on a snowy surface. After a fresh fall of snow, everything has a white top edge and you must leave space for this when painting. Snow is rarely completely white as it reflects the colour of the sky and other strong features. Very few areas are white in the finished painting on page 21.

If you are painting in the snow remember to wear plenty of warm clothing. You will soon find it too cold to work even if you are making no more than a thirty-minute sketch.

Demonstration

Size: 265 × 203 mm/10½ × 8 in.
Brushes: 0, 1, 2 sable. Paper: Bockingford 285 gsm/140 lb.

Stage 1

Draw the outline of the lower edge of the sky where it meets the details of the landscape. Wet the sky area and lay in washes mixed from hooker's green, ultramarine and crimson red. Keep these extremely pale without hard edges.

Stage 2

When the sky is dry begin work on the bridge and houses on either side with a mixture of raw umber and sepia with Prussian blue. Leave patches of white on the roof-tops and along the top of the bridge for a layer of snow. Use a mixture of sepia and Prussian blue for the darker shadowy areas on the buildings and under the bridge, and for the shadow of the bridge in the water.

The features in this stage are all hard shapes, so the drawing and perspective must be correct. Nearly all the other features of the landscape allow a certain amount of artistic licence, but the man-made structures must look realistic.

Stage 3

Indicate the distant trees beyond the bridge, using dry-brush to paint delicate shades of hooker's green, ultramarine and crimson red, raw umber and sepia. Leave the uppermost parts of the trees white for snow. When the foliage is dry, put in shadowy trunks and branches with diluted sepia.

Make a very pale wash from ultramarine and crimson red and lay a shadow across the roof of the house on the right.

Stage 4

Draw in the edge of the river bank in the foreground. Put in a dark area of shadow for the overhung area

Study the tonal values. The sky is not the lightest tone of all, as on a bright summer day.

with a mixture of raw umber, sepia and Prussian blue. Keep the edges of this hard to give a jagged effect. The river reflects the colours of the sky and the trees and foliage on its banks. Use a wash mixed from ultramarine and crimson red for the river surface in the distance. Paint in the mass of undergrowth on the left bank with burnt sienna, ultramarine and raw umber to give the effect of a tangled mass. Blend the sepia wash into the river with water to create the correct reflection.

Stage 1

Stage 2

Stage 3

Stage 4

Complete the water surface by using a very pale wash of hooker's green and ultramarine. Use sap green, sepia and Prussian blue to paint the conifers on the right. Study the brushwork for these trees: the angle of the brushstroke as much as the colour makes the trees look like conifers.

Stage 5

Add fine details to the buildings and their stonework to give them character. Give shape and form to the snow-covered foreground with washes of hooker's green and ultramarine and include a few dashes of sepia wash around the edge of the river bank.

Stage 5 - the finished painting

Finally, paint in the bare saplings in the lower left-and right-hand corners of the painting with the same colours as for the foliage on the left-hand side of the bridge on the opposite bank. Do not make these lines of paint too dark or the effect will be too heavy against the snow.

Hooker's green and ultramarine, although originating in the sky, are reflected in all the light areas throughout the painting. This gives an overall unity to the work.

Rocky ravine

Size: 265 × 265 mm/10½ × 10½ in.
Brushes: 0, 1, 2, 6 sable. Paper: Bockingford 285 gsm/
140 lb.

Rocky headlands, steep cliffs, highland outcrops and
rough boulders are good subjects. Angular outlines and
sharp shadows together with a wide range of colours
and textures give opportunity for experimentation and
a combination of different techniques.

Practise these techniques on a spare sheet of paper
before attempting a finished picture. Apply pigment
very loosely with a large brush and lots of water. Let
the paint produce its own shapes and patterns as it
dries. Create interesting textural effects and highlights
by gently lifting out the colour from certain areas with
a clean sponge, rag or paper tissue while the paint is
still wet. Wash colour from dry areas by first applying
water to loosen the pigment. Use stippling techniques
to create rough textures. Apply colour with minimal
water and use a large brush. Colour applied in this way
can always be manipulated afterwards if you use more
water to blend and soften tones. Notice the contrasts
between areas where two or more colours have been
applied separately using this technique and areas treat-
ed with the same colours mixed previously on the pal-
ette and applied together as one wash.

Demonstration

Stage 1

Establish the outline of the glimpse of sky at the top
of the picture by drawing the silhouette of the stone
footbridge above the waterfall and the rough wall leading away from it to the right. Wet the sky area and lay
in a wash of very pale yellow ochre, thus emphasizing
the darker areas of colour at the edge of the sky. Put
a slight amount of ultramarine in the centre of the sky
to give an impression of pale blue among the light
clouds. For the shadow under the bridge use a mixture
of sepia and Prussian blue and add the shape of the
dark distant forest with the same colours. Let the paint
dry.

Stage 2

Isolate the outcrops of rock and establish the outline
of the waterfall and ravine. This is the most important
stage of the whole painting as these stony features
provide the backbone for a wide range of colour and
textural effects. Lay in these areas with varying proportions of sepia and Prussian blue. Keep some edges
hard and blend others off with water where the undergrowth overhangs them. Lift out areas of colour to give
some tonal variation. Do not apply the paint too thickly: it is always better to make a wash too thin rather
than too heavy. Let all these areas of paint dry
thoroughly.

Stage 3

Now begin work on the trees and foliage at the top of
the ravine. Use sap green, sepia and burnt sienna. Wet
small patches of the paper and softly paint in these
colours. Let the paper dry and then use drybrush for
a leafy effect and encourage the development of a

speckled light from behind the foliage. I have used different brushstrokes for different types of foliage. Practise short dabbing brushstrokes with a no. 1 sable for the effect of the coniferous tree directly in front of the footbridge.

Stage 4

For wet grass and moss on either side of the waterfall, use sap green, hooker's green, yellow ochre and raw umber in varying wash proportions above the rocks. Wet patches of the paper to allow these colours to merge into one another and let them flow over the tops of some parts of rock to give a realistic overgrown look. Small speckled patches of white paper show through these washes and are important to the overall effect of the painting.

Stage 5 (detail shown on back cover)

Complete the painting with very thin washes of ultramarine and sepia to produce the waterfall, the stonework on the bridge and the rocks leading away to the right. Put in some ferns on the right-hand bank with drybrush and sap green, burnt sienna and Prussian blue.

    The pleasing effect of this painting is mainly due to the strong feeling of light emerging from behind the bridge and passing through the trees but not quite penetrating into the moist, dark depths of the ravine.

Tonal study of the finished painting on page 25

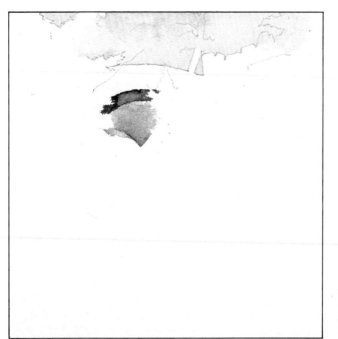

Stage 1

Stage 2

Stage 3

Stage 4

Stage 5 - the finished painting

Sky.
Ultramarine

Pale Blue
Blue Green

Blue/Grey

Raw Umber/
Burnt Sienna

Dk Blue/Grey

Dark Grn/
Hookers

Green
Sienna

Ochre

Green.

Sienna/Crimson

Purple/Ochre
Crimson

Green/Sienna

Dark Brown/Red
Prussian Blue

Dry Grasses
Ochre/Raw Umber.

If you see something you would like to paint but do not have your watercolour equipment with you, make an annotated pencil sketch (like the one above) and note colour details on the drawing. Although this sketch looks quite thorough, I made it very quickly. Before putting pencil to paper, I considered exactly what I wanted to draw and isolated the basic tonal areas. I completed this drawing in seven and a half minutes and added some colour notes as accurately as possible.

26

Watercolour sketching

The demonstration on page 11, *Gloomy weather*, shows how useful it is to be able to work quickly. It is essential, for instance, when painting a sunset where lighting effects change rapidly. Detail can be important, but too much attention to it can make work look over-intense and unattractive. I taught myself to draw quickly by setting myself a specific time within which to complete a drawing. I still do this now and again to keep in practice. It is always a good idea to draw as much as you can, but now and again you should set yourself a time target for a satisfactory drawing. Attention to detail will suffer, but your ability to capture an accurate impression on paper will improve rapidly. I often find that a quick impression is more vivid and true to my intention than a ponderously detailed work.

Demonstration

Size: 265 × 190 mm/10½ × 7½ in.
Brushes: 1, 2, 4 sable. Paper: Bockingford 285 gsm/140 lb.

Stage 1

Make a fine pencil drawing of the cloud shapes and establish the horizon on the paper. Paint the sky with broken wash of ultramarine, Prussian blue and hooker's green. Vary the tone to produce uneven patches of light.

Stage 2

Colour in the tall buildings and roof-tops, and distant fields that catch the sunlight. Mix Prussian blue, crimson red and sepia for the shadows which the buttresses cast on the walls. This is a sketch and not a painting, so do not spend too much time trying to obtain perfect hard or soft edges on each area of colour. Let all these light parts dry.

Stage 3

Add the clusters of trees on the hillside, the thin conifers and full deciduous trees in the middle distance. Use sap green, sepia and Prussian blue with touches of burnt sienna. If the green trees are too heavy, lift out some wet colour with a clean brush as I have done just below the tall central building. While the paint is still drying, lightly pencil in the foreground details.

Stage 1

Stage 2

Stage 3

Stage 4

Stage 4

Make up thin washes of yellow ochre, sap green and burnt sienna and lay in the low-lying fields on either side of the river. A few dark horizontals give greater distance to the trees and buildings. Paint the river with the colours you used for the sky in stage 1.

Stage 5

Complete the painting with bold brushstrokes of raw umber, yellow ochre and burnt sienna for the rows of stubble and dry grasses in the foreground. If you apply the paint too thickly the effect will be too heavy.

This is not an outstanding painting, but a successful sketch (it took less than half an hour).

Stage 5 - the finished painting

Composition

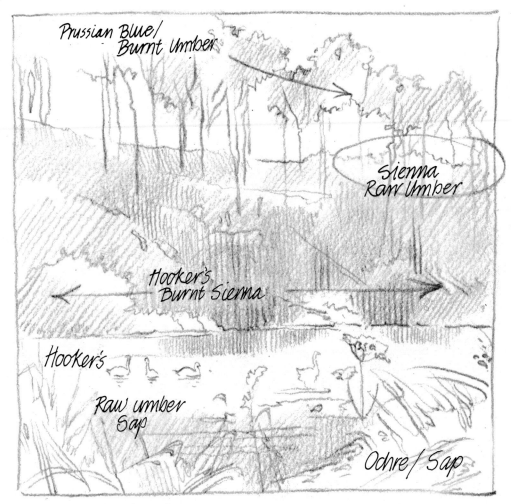

Prussian Blue/
Burnt Umber

Sienna
Raw Umber

Hooker's
Burnt Sienna

Hooker's

Raw umber
Sap

Ochre / Sap

Basic errors of composition always stand out. Five minutes spent on a quick sketch or plan is rarely wasted. Many mistakes are hard to detect in the mind's eye, but once on paper in sketch form they can soon be eliminated.

The strong horizontals in this composition would seem too dominant in a traditional landscape format, but are appropriate to a square shape.

The original scene for the top drawing appeared exactly like this. I made a new drawing (below) with the basic composition altered. I left out the barbed wire fence, made the farmhouse larger, and gently curved the cart track further to the right.

ACKNOWLEDGMENTS

Painting Landscapes in Watercolour.

Text, drawings and paintings by Jan Burridge.

First published in Great Britain in 1981
Search Press Limited, Wellwood, North Farm Road,
Tunbridge Wells, Kent TN2 3DR.

Text, illustrations, arrangement and typography
copyright © Search Press Limited 1981.

Reprinted 1982, 1984, 1985, 1986, 1987, 1989

U.S. Artists Materials Trade Distributor:
Winsor & Newton, Inc.
P. O. Box 1519, 555 Winsor Drive, Secaucus,
NJ 07094

Canadian Distributors:
Anthes Universal Limited
341 Heart Lake Road South, Brampton, Ontario
L6W 3K8

Australian Distributors:
Jasco Pty. Limited
937-941 Victoria Road, West Ryde, N.S.W. 2114

New Zealand Distributors:
Caldwell Wholesale Ltd
Wellington and Auckland

ISBN 0 85532 441 4

Made and printed in Spain by A. G. Elkar, S. Coop.
Autonomía, 71 - 48012-Bilbao - Spain.

Detail from the finished painting on page 17